SHARKS
AN IMAGINATION LIBRARY SERIES

VERY BIG SHARKS

by Victor Gentle and Janet Perry

**Gareth Stevens Publishing**
A WORLD ALMANAC EDUCATION GROUP COMPANY

Please visit our web site at: www.garethstevens.com
For a free color catalog describing Gareth Stevens' list of high-quality books and
multimedia programs, call 1-800-542-2595 (USA) or 1-800-461-9120 (Canada).
Gareth Stevens Publishing's Fax: (414) 332-3567.

Library of Congress Cataloging-in-Publication Data

Gentle, Victor.
    Very big sharks / by Victor Gentle and Janet Perry.
        p. cm. — (Sharks: an imagination library series)
    Includes bibliographical references and index.
    ISBN 0-8368-2828-3 (lib. bdg.)
    1. Sharks—Juvenile literature. [1. Sharks.] I. Perry, Janet, 1960-  II. Title.
    QL638.9.G359   2001
    597.3—dc21                                          00-052246

First published in 2001 by
**Gareth Stevens Publishing**
A World Almanac Education Group Company
330 West Olive Street, Suite 100
Milwaukee, WI  53212  USA

Text: Victor Gentle and Janet Perry
Page layout: Victor Gentle, Janet Perry, and Scott Krall
Cover design: Scott Krall
Series editor: Heidi Sjostrom
Picture Researcher: Diane Laska-Swanke

Photo credits: Cover, © Ron & Valerie Taylor/Innerspace Visions; p. 5 (main)
© Mark Strickland/Innerspace Visions; p. 5 (inset) © Gwen Lowe/Innerspace Visions;
p. 7 © Howard Hall/Innerspace Visions; p. 9 (main) © Chip Clark, NMNH, Smithsonian
Institution; p. 9 (inset) © Bob Cranston/Innerspace Visions; p. 11 © Doug Perrine/Innerspace
Visions; p. 13 © George W. Benz/Innerspace Visions; p. 15 © Amos Nachoum/Innerspace
Visions; p. 17 © Gary Adkison/Innerspace Visions; p. 19 © A & A Ferrari/Innerspace Visions;
p. 21 © Bruce Rasner/Innerspace Visions

Printed in the United States of America

1 2 3 4 5 6 7 8 9 05 04 03 02 01

*Front cover:* A massive whale shark and
diver swim in the ocean near Australia.

# TABLE OF CONTENTS

Words that appear in the glossary are printed in **boldface** type the first time they occur in the text.

# HOW BIG IS A SHARK?

Ask your friends how big sharks are. They will probably tell you, "Big — twice as long as a person, or even bigger." True, some **species** of sharks are big, but many species are small. We know of 400 species of sharks. More than half these species grow to less than 4 feet (1.2 meters). Only about 15 species get longer than 13 feet (4 m), or about twice the length of Michael Jordan.

This book is about the really big species — our "top ten." Nine are alive. One is **extinct**.

Warning: new discoveries might change the order on the list. Shark size charts also depend on the measurements the chart makers choose to believe.

*Main photo*: The whale shark is the largest living fish of any kind. It can grow to 40 feet (12.2 m) long for sure, and possibly as long as 60 feet (18.3 m), according to one report. *Inset*: By contrast, the pygmy shark, one of the smallest sharks in the world, reaches only about ten inches (25.4 centimeters) when it is fully grown.

# THE GENTLE GIANTS

The whale shark and the basking shark are the gentle giants of the shark world. They are harmless to humans, but don't try to fit them into a pool.

The whale shark is the largest shark alive. On average, whale sharks grow to be about 30 feet (9.1 m) long.

Basking sharks are usually just a few inches (cm) shorter than the whale shark. The longest reliably reported basking shark was 40 feet (12.2 m) long.

Both the whale shark and the basking shark feed on **plankton,** small **crustaceans** (like **krill** and shrimp), and small fish. They never attack people.

The basking shark is second in our ranking of the world's biggest living sharks. To sift out its food, a basking shark strains tons of water through its **gill rakers**.

# A PREHISTORIC MONSTER

Possibly the biggest species of shark ever was *Carcharodon megalodon*. This prehistoric monster probably has been extinct for over four million years, so we must study fossils to learn about it.

*Carcharodon megalodon* is an ancient relative of the white shark, the most feared man-eating shark alive today (see page 14). The name *Carcharodon megalodon* means "rough tooth, big tooth."

Trying to guess from a few **fossilized** teeth, scientists think that *Carcharodon megalodon* may have grown to about 43 feet (13.1 m) long. The largest ones may have been bigger than this. If they were alive today, they could easily swallow the largest white sharks.

These model jaws of a *Carcharodon megalodon* are on exhibit at the Smithsonian Institution in Washington, DC. The teeth are three times larger than the white shark's teeth.

# TIGER, TIGER, BITING TIGHT

Unlike the whale shark and the basking shark, the tiger shark is dangerous to larger forms of sea life. Its heavy, **serrated** teeth and powerful jaws can slice through the bodies and shells of large sea turtles.

At times, tiger sharks swim along **tropical** shores. They have been known to eat pigs, donkeys, cows, and sheep that get swept out to sea. They have also been known to attack a few humans who have fallen overboard into the sea.

For sure, tiger sharks can grow to a length of 18 feet (5.5 m). Several people have even reported seeing tiger sharks that were up to 24 feet (7.3 m) long — and longer. That makes the tiger shark the third largest living shark on our size chart.

Many people think the tiger shark is the most dangerous shark in the world. Most sea turtles, seals, and sea lions would probably agree. In turn, tiger sharks are food for people.

# THE BIG SLEEPERS

Sleeper sharks are a mysterious group of sharks that usually live in deep, very cold water. Two species of sleeper sharks make it into the top ten biggest sharks in the world that we know about.

The Pacific sleeper shark reaches 23 feet (7 m), making it number 4 on the shark size chart. The Greenland shark weighs in at over a ton (1,016 kilograms) and grows to about 21 feet (6.4 m), so it is number 6 on the largest-living-sharks list.

Greenland sharks eat fish and seals. Fishers catch many Greenland sharks with small **parasites** on their eyes. The parasites glow in the deep, dark waters. Fishers think these glowing critters guide **prey** into the sharks' mouths. Even sharks use night-lights!

The Greenland shark is the smaller of the two big sleeper sharks. This one was caught in the sea off Baffin Island, Canada. Its eye is infected with a parasitic **copepod**.

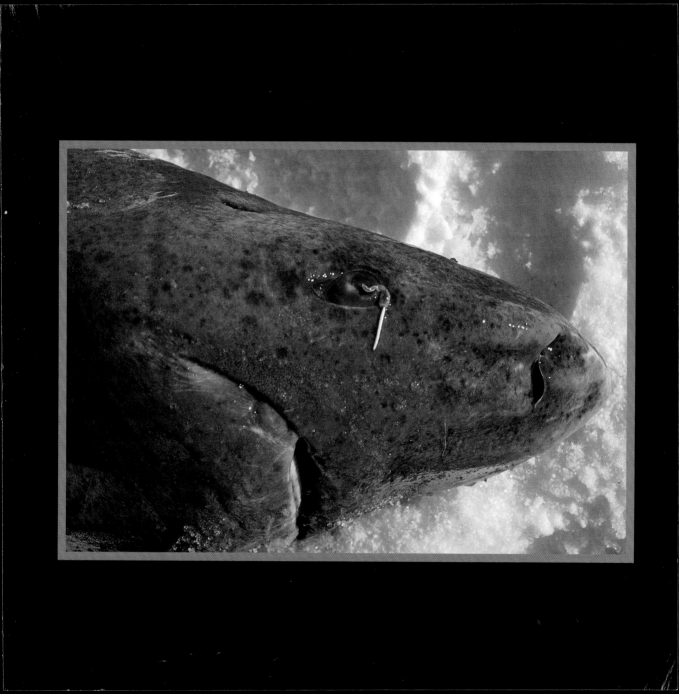

# WHITE DEATH

The white shark — also called white death or the great white shark — is the modern cousin of the long extinct *Carcharodon megalodon*. About half the size of their prehistoric relatives, white sharks can grow to over 21 feet (6.4 m) in length. We rank the white shark number 5 on our living sharks size chart.

White sharks are the most ferocious animals in the ocean. They eat only about once a week, but they get to eat just about anything they want! Their jaws are six times stronger than a wolf's jaws, and have about two-thirds the biting strength of a *Tyrannosaurus rex*'s jaws. White sharks are responsible for making a third to a half of all deadly attacks on humans.

The white shark has been hunted hard since it gained world-wide fame as the villain in the book and movie *Jaws*. The species is now so endangered that many countries protect it.

# GREAT HAMMERHEAD

Great hammerhead sharks can grow to 20 feet (6.1 m) in length. They are the largest of the eight species in the hammerhead shark family.

No one knows for sure why they have **evolved** their special head shapes, with their eyes on the ends of two large, flattened side parts. Hammerheads also have extra large nostrils.

The great hammerhead shark eats a wide range of fish, including other sharks. It has also, on a few occasions, been known to attack humans.

The great hammerhead has the same maximum length as the common thresher shark, but it is heavier. So we have ranked the hammerhead number 7 on our living sharks size chart!

Hammerhead sharks have a wide-ranging taste in food. They have even been seen attacking and eating other sharks — including other hammerhead sharks.

# TAILS 'R' US

When you rank sharks by length, the thresher shark is up there, but only by cheating a little. If it didn't have that incredibly long tail, it would be way down on the list. However, nothing in our rule book says that extra long shark tails don't count!

A thresher shark's tail is almost as long as the rest of its body. The longest thresher on record is 20 feet (6.1 m). That's 1,000 pounds (454 kg) of shark. It's number 8 on our chart.

Threshers use their tails to slap the water and force their prey — **shoals** of fish, for example — into tight groups. Then they turn quickly and swim through the tightly bunched fish, swallowing large numbers with each pass.

Although some people on fishing boats have reported attacks by threshers, the International Shark Attack File lists only one direct attack on a human by a thresher in the past 350 years.

# BIGMOUTH

Number 9 on our list of the biggest known living sharks is the megamouth shark. The first megamouth was discovered in 1976, near Hawaii. Thirteen more were sighted by the year 2000. The biggest one measured is about 17 feet (5.2 m) long.

So far, we know very little about this strange shark. Megamouths live in the open ocean, usually in very deep water. Like whale sharks and basking sharks, megamouths feed on plankton and other small sea animals, including shrimp and jellyfish. They don't seem to be dangerous to people.

If a shark as big as this was discovered only within the past thirty years, how many more surprises do the oceans hold in store for us?

This is a rare megamouth shark. A few years ago, another one was spotted being attacked by sperm whales off the coast of Indonesia.

# MORE TO READ AND VIEW

**Books (Nonfiction)**   *Eugenie Clark: Adventures of a Shark Scientist.* Ellen R. Butts and
Joyce R. Schwartz (Shoe String Press)
*The Really Sinister Savage Shark and other Creatures of the Deep. The
Really Horrible Guides* (series). Barbara Taylor (DK Publishing)
*Shark Attack. Real Kids, Real Adventures* (series). Deborah Morris
(Berkley Publishing Group)
*Sharks* (series). Victor Gentle and Janet Perry (Gareth Stevens)

**Books (Activity)**   *Eyewitness Activity File: Shark.* Deni Bown (DK Publishing)

**Books (Fiction)**   *The Escape (Animorphs #15).* K. A. Applegate (Scholastic)
*The Shark Callers.* Eric Campbell (Harcourt Brace)
*Swimming with Sharks.* Twig C. George (HarperCollins)
*'Ula Li'i and the Magic Shark.* Donivee Martin Laird (Barnaby Books)

**Videos (Nonfiction)**   *Hunt for the Great White Shark.* (National Geographic)
*National Geographic's The Sharks.* (National Geographic)
*National Geographic's Treasures of the Deep.* (National Geographic)
*Vanishing Wonders of the Sea.* (Sumeria)

# PLACES TO WRITE AND VISIT

Here are three places to contact for more information:

| | | |
|---|---|---|
| Greenpeace | World Wildlife Fund | Vancouver Aquarium |
| 702 H Street NW | 1250 24th Street NW, Suite 500 | P.O. Box 3232 |
| Washington, DC 20001 | Washington, DC 20037 | Vancouver, BC |
| USA | USA | Canada V6B 3X8 |
| 1-202-462-1177 | 1-800-CALL-WWF | 1-604-659-3474 |
| **www.greenpeace.org** | **www.wwf.org** | |

To find a zoo or aquarium to visit, check out **www.aza.org** and, on the American Zoo and
Aquarium's home page, look under <u>AZA Services</u>, and click on <u>Find a Zoo or Aquarium</u>.

# WEB SITES

If you have your own computer and Internet access, great! If not, most libraries have Internet access. The Internet changes every day, and web sites come and go. We believe the sites we recommend here are likely to last, and that they give the best and most appropriate links for our readers to pursue their interest in sharks and their environment.

**www.ajkids.com**
This is the junior Ask Jeeves site — it's a great research tool. Some questions to try out in Ask Jeeves Kids:

> Which sharks eat each other?

> What are sharks' worst enemies?

You can also just type in words and phrases with "?" at the end, for example:

> Protecting sharks?

> Shark fossils?

**www.flmnh.ufl.edu/fish/sharks/statistics/ GAttack/mapusa.htm**
Shark Attack Map of the USA. Look at the columns where the numbers are. Notice the places where attacks occur most often.

**www.mbayaq.org/lc/kids_place/kidseq.asp**
This is the Kids' E-quarium of the Monterey Bay Aquarium. Make postcards, print out coloring pages, play games, go on a virtual deep-sea dive, or find out about some marine science careers.

**kids.discovery.com/KIDS**
Click on the Live SharkCam. See a live leopard shark and live blacktip reef sharks!

**oberon.educ.sfu.ca/splash/tank.htm**
It's the Touch Tank. Click on a critter or a rock in the aquarium to see more about it. If you have Quicktime, it'll be animated. Cool!

**www2.orbit.net.mt/sharkman/index.htm**
Enter the Sharkman's World near Malta. He's a scuba diver who is completely soaked in anything even a little bit sharky. You'll find poetry, music, and shark pictures there. The Sharkman is not a scientist, but he loves to talk sharks with other shark fans — like you!

**www.pbs.org/wgbh/nova/sharks/world/ clickable.html**
It's the Clickable Shark. Click on any part of the shark picture to find out how sharks work.

**www.pbs.org/wgbh/nova/sharks/world/ whoswho.html**
Here's a shark "family tree." Click on any of the titles, and you'll see what kinds of sharks belong in the same group, and why. If you see a picture of a shark you don't know, use the Shark-O-Matic to get answers.

# GLOSSARY

You can find these words on the pages listed.  Reading a word in a sentence helps you understand it even better.

**copepod** (KOHP-ah-pod) — one of the tiny animals in a subgroup of crustaceans  12

**crustaceans** (krus-TAE-shuns) — animals with outer skeletons that protect their bodies like suits of armor  6

**evolved** (ee-VOLVED) — changed gradually over time to better suit the surroundings  16

**extinct** (ex-TINKT) — with no more members of that species left alive  4, 8, 14

**fossilized** (FAH-sill-ized) — in the form of ancient living things found in shapes, traces, or remains left in rocks  8

**gill rakers** — rows of bristles, near some sharks' gills, that filter sea water to get the small animals and plants that sharks eat  6

**gills** — the breathing parts of sharks and other fish; gills take in oxygen from the water  24

**krill** — tiny shrimp-like crustaceans that swarm in vast numbers in the ocean  6

**parasites** (PAR-ah-sites) — creatures that live on other creatures, using their nutrients  12

**plankton** (PLANK-ton) — tiny animals and plants that drift in the ocean  6, 20

**prey** (PRAY) — animals that are hunted for food  12, 18

**serrated** (SAIR-ate-ed) — with wavy or toothed edges  10

**shoals** (SHOLES) — groups of fish of the same species swimming together  18

**species** (SPEE-shees) — a group of plants or animals that are very alike  4, 8, 12, 14, 16

**tropical** (TRAH-pi-cul) — from the wide area of warm lands and seas near the equator  10

# INDEX